THERE IS HEALING
And Life After

RESOURCES

Elisabeth Kübler-Ross Theory, Used by permission. All rights reserved

All direct Bible quotes were taken from the King James Version (KJV) and the New International version (NIV), public domain accessed 6/12/2021.

Editor: Rhea Edmonds
Cover: Your Vision Design (Sheila Collins)

ISBN 979-8-9851544-1-2

DEDICATIONS

This Book is dedicated to my loved ones who I refer to as “always remembered" and “never forgotten". They are resting and awaiting the trumpet sound on that great day! They are the pillars in my life that have provided the stability and soundness that has pushed me to write my first of many books.

Mom and Dad there is not a day that passes when I do not think about the both of you and if you were still here how you would be during this time. Dad we spoke on the phone daily and your intellect, sound advice and wisdom has allowed me to keep pushing no matter what. You never gave up nor did you make excuses. Instead, you adjusted and always found a way to make it work. Mom your prayers have carried me through and when I begin to feel faint in heart I am reminded of your words of encouragement and can even still see that beautiful smile on your lovely face. I was blessed with two of the most wonderful loving and caring parents any child could have. Thank you for pouring into me so I could pay it forward by pouring out and into someone else. You both taught me so much. I am forever grateful and inspired by your Love and how you gave so much of yourselves so that your seed could be better!

To my wonderful husband, my lover, my friend, my earthly Pastor, and advisor, you were so many things to me and for me. We talked about the many plans we had to travel and to grow old together, but our Sovereign God had another plan. As I reflect on our conversations now, it is so clear to me that you were preparing me for this even if you did not realize it. There was that gut feeling that your time of departure was drawing near. You will always be a part of my life because I see you in our children and our grandchildren. Our son Wayne is a wonderful Pastor just like you always knew he would be! Your legacy still remains and for that I could not be happier! I have no regrets. We will see each other again in the Morning! Keep resting my sweetness.

Last but not least my first-born son, Wesley Adell Moore II. What can I say but how thankful I am to have been able to birth you – a Praiser and a Worshipper! While carrying you my praise and worship for God was consistent so it did not surprise me that it became your life. Wesley your children each have a piece of you so we can be assured that you are still with us through each of them! Wesley III is the Worshipper just like you. Music is in his bones. Destiny is funny, comical, and always teasing her brothers- sound familiar? She also has your mood swings, and she is not a morning person! Oh, how well I remember you not being a morning person either. And then there's Jordan the athlete. He loves sports and he even loves playing the drums. He is your happy go lucky child with such an even and mild temperament.

So even though you have transitioned, we are able to be reminded of you when we see your beautiful children. Son we all miss you a lot yet by God's strength we are still moving forward moment by moment. Rest in Jesus.

ACKNOWLEDGMENTS

When my life appeared to be turned upside down, I saw my only remaining son Wayne become a giant right before my eyes. He declared that I would not have to worry and that he would be available for me whenever I needed him. Wayne, you have been a stellar son in your caring and looking out for me. Even when I would tell myself to not bother Wayne with that (whatever that was at the time) it was as if you already knew so you would be right there in the nick of time. Thank you for loving me and always covering me. It is as if our roles have shifted and now, you are in charge of me! As we say to each other every time we talk, "I Love You". Your Mama Bear

Finally, I must take the time to recognize a wonderful woman of God who has been a part of this book writing & editing process who I refer to as my editor. She has read the drafts (yes plural) repeatedly. She has corrected and provided thought provoking parallels which have stretched me in my writing skills. And she is such a pleasant and patient individual.

Rhea Edmonds I cannot thank you enough for your efforts and the time and late hours you have put into perfecting my story for God's glory! May God reward you exceedingly and abundantly more than you could ever ask or think. Your selfless sacrifices on my behalf have not gone unnoticed. Thank you from the bottom of my heart. I thank God for our friendship.

FOREWORD
By Bishop Annie Njeri

In this book **"There is Healing and Life After,"** Pastor Charlotte has shared her personal life story and love of her family. She has explained how one should allow himself/herself to grieve using the seven words "there is no wrong way to grieve."

Charlotte has explained with such conviction that *there is healing and life after* which I can testify that she has received spiritual healing and have closely watched her life take a drastic turn in a positive way having taken a major decision to carry on with life and ministry even after the death of her husband Bishop Wesley Moore. You will discover her revealing her bedroom talks with her late husband Bishop Wesley telling her "You must fulfil your God given purpose on earth" and how they exchanged words of love daily. Everybody has a purpose and destiny to fulfil but most women think that their calling is only to be helpmates to their spouses. (Genesis 2:18) But I agree with Pastor Charlotte that you need to pursue and fulfil your purpose on earth.

I personally knew Bishop Wesley and the year he transitioned they were scheduled to come to London UK as our guest speakers for our annual conference, International Gathering of Nation Changers (IGNC). When l heard the news my first expression was how will Pastor Charlotte survive without Bishop by her side? This couple was a true example of true love for husband and wife, and l can only describe them as having fitted in each other's lives as a hand and glove.

I thank God for healing Pastor Charlotte. Well-done Pastor for allowing God's love to penetrate through you and in your life. Thank you for your honesty that many times you were vulnerable to and just wanted to cry. As you face the next chapter in your life, you will bless many lives with this true-life story.

I recommend you read every word in this book carefully. Allow yourself to heal. Yes, "there is no wrong way to grieve" but remember "There is Healing and Life After". Be healed, arise, and fulfil your God given purpose.

Bishop Annie Njeri, Senior Pastor

Airport Church Revival Centre, Feltham UK

CEO/Founder Brooks of Life Ministries International

FOREWORD

By Dr Sandy Burkett, PhD

I met Pastor Charlotte in 2006 when she became a student of Breakthrough Biblical Counseling training. During her time as a student I was impressed, as a Pastor, with her vulnerability. I witnessed a passion in her heart to help others become free of their life issues. During that time, I witnessed a level of respect in her heart and love of people. She was humble and powerful at the same time.

When Pastor Charlotte's husband died, her world was turned upside down, inside out and twisted with confusion, agony, and wanting to give up being used by God. Daily her pain shouted louder than her purpose.

Through the prayers of others Pastor Charlotte began to understand that pain is inevitable, but suffering is optional. She came back as a student in 2015 to obtain tools for herself to live a life of victory. Charlotte moved from being a victim to a survivor then to an overcomer. As an overcomer she has had women weep on her shoulders, she has helped them to stand and sometimes gently pushed them out of the nest to move on their own. Her life transformation is a witness of the power of the Living God to those that want to give up and have lost their dream.

Apostle Sandy Burkett, PhD.
She with her husband Pastor Greg are founders of Breakthrough Reconciliation and Breakthrough Biblical Counseling. Dr. Sandy has been in ministry since 1980.

She has ministered in the United States, Ukraine, and Haiti. She is co-author of *Healing the Wounds That Hold You Back* and *Healing Your Soul*.

CONTENTS

PREFACE

I always knew that someday I would have the opportunity to write a few books. And what came to mind were books related to teaching and training which I plan to do. However, I never imagined that my first book would be sharing a portion of my life's story and survival. I never thought I would be writing about some of the people near and dear to me that would no longer be here and that they would become the reason for this book existing. Life has some interesting twists and turns where sometimes those turns do not look like we envisioned.

To say this was easy would be very inaccurate and an understatement on my part. The people that cared for me, loved me, provided for me, and have strongly contributed to who I am today are all a part of my story, yet they are no longer here.

If there is anything I can say to you it would be to cherish the 'time' you have with your loved ones because once they are gone, you can never get that 'time' back. Make sure you live with no regrets. Be quick to apologize and to forgive. Above all do not sweat the small stuff because life is too short. We all know that death is a part of life, but it is not meant to stop you from living life after a loved one is gone. Even they would want you to live your life to the fullest because there is still "Life" after.

It is my Prayer that as you read 'my journey' that you will be able to embrace and accept the things that you have personally been faced with in life. Make the necessary adjustments and become responsible in deciding how you will allow your personal journey to define you. Will it make you or will it break you? Will you choose to become 'better' or 'bitter'? I made the choice to become a much better person in the midst of my circumstances and guess what? So can you!

REFLECTIONS

As I reflect on my mom, I see someone who has endured and overcome.

I have watched her life, and I have seen how she has handled life's mountains, peaks, and the valleys, yet she has overcome. I have witnessed her walk in her roles as a mother, wife, sister, minister, first lady, evangelist, and mentor. While wearing these hats she has had to endure many things, but I believe she was graced to not just go through but to overcome in every situation.

If you live long enough you will go through, but you need to also know that you can overcome! My mother's life is a true example of an OVERCOMER!

Wayne A. Moore Sr

If you have ever had someone pour into you until your soul is refreshed, then you would have an idea of who Evangelist Charlotte Moore is and what she means to me. For over 15 years she has been my spiritual mom, mentor, and friend. She has seen and listened to me when my life was broken. Without judgment, she gave me compassion and sound advice. I know countless others who can say the same thing.

She shares her knowledge and experiences freely, and in doing so makes our lives better for knowing her. The love of Christ that I have received through this vessel of God has helped heal and develop my walk with God. I am eternally grateful to God for placing her in my life. Her examples of faithfulness, perseverance, commitment, and integrity are inspiring, and I understand Paul's statement, "Follow me as I follow Christ." To follow Charlotte Moore, is to follow Christ, for her mind is made up and her eyes are on the prize.

Thank you, Mom, for allowing your light to shine!

Ladell Jones

PROCESSING THE GRIEF

What does it mean to be healed? Let's look at the definition of the word. Merriam-Webster's dictionary meaning for ‘heal' is to make sound or whole, to make well again, to restore to health. So healing is always possible, no matter what a person needs to be healed from.

People often want to know when and how long - how long it will take and when they will know that they are healed.

It must be felt before it is seen, meaning healing must first come from within, which has to do with how a person thinks and his or her ability and willingness to accept the need for healing.

When my husband passed away, I thought the trauma of his loss was the only thing I needed to be healed from; however, as time passed, I learned that his passing was only one part of the process. There were layers of healing with which I needed to deal.

"How do I live now?"
"What will I do without him?"
"Could I have saved his life?"
"Why did he leave me?"
"Why did God take him from me?

So many questions...not enough answers. When people grieve, their minds go in a multitude of directions - right or wrong - looking for something or someone to blame. They often want to recall if their final words were sweet or bitter. Yes, all of this becomes part of the healing process.

I remember it like it was yesterday. I was leaving my home to visit and care for my parents. My dad was expecting a house call from Home Health Care, so I needed to be at their home when the healthcare worker arrived. As I prepared to go to my car, I heard my husband, Wesley, calling my name. I figured he wanted me to bring him something before I exited. Since I was leaving earlier than usual, I was in no hurry.

Then he called for me a second time, but this time as I heard him, there was a difference in his voice – desperation. I immediately went upstairs to our bedroom, and he was sitting on the side of the bed. "I can't breathe," he said. I asked, "Are you in pain?" He replied, "No, I'm just having difficulty breathing." I immediately dialed 911, and then I went back to his side, prayed, and proceeded to see if there was anything I could do to help him. There was nothing. I was helpless. As we waited for the paramedics to arrive, I was still being prayerful. We had said, "I love you," to each other as always. The difference this time was not knowing that those words would be the final three words I would say to my husband of nearly 40 years.

Losing my spouse was a pain that pierced a place inside me that hurt in unimaginable ways. I had experienced the loss of three siblings along with other family members and close friends. This loss, however, was a much deeper hurt - - a hurt that I did not know how to fix. It was as if a part of my heart was gone, a part that I would never get back. So how was I to deal with this?

A person must be honest enough with himself or herself to admit that he or she is hurting so he or she can properly 'heal' and become healthy again. Is that easy? No, it is not because in that moment one must admit the need for healing. Sometimes we would rather remain in a state of denial than to admit that we need help. That place of denial becomes our safety net. It keeps us from having to deal with the pain of what has happened. However, we cannot remain in that state forever and be healed and healthy.

I mentioned earlier the layers of healing that must take place after a loss - any loss - death, divorce, job, property, house, car, etc. For me, it was the loss of my husband, Wesley. We did everything together, and at times we thought as 'one' - like knowing what the other person was thinking to the point of finishing each other's sentences. We had a very special bond. He was the love of my life, my true soul mate. When I married Wesley, I did not just repeat the marriage vows. I meant them. When I said, 'I do,' it was for better or worse, richer, or poorer, in sickness and health, until death. But I was not prepared for the latter -- death parting us. Not now! Not yet!

Someone once said, "We are often taught how to gain and receive, but we are never taught how to lose and let go." So how does one prepare to lose a loved one? Honestly speaking, we don't. Loss teaches us. I know you probably were not expecting that answer, but you already knew, didn't you? There are no lessons, no book of instructions to read about how to prepare your feelings to adjust/accept a loss. May I be honest?

Since everyone is different, the response to loss will also be different - not wrong, just different. I was given some of the best advice I had ever received when my husband passed. Again, it was not given to me while he was living; it was after his departure. That lets me know that this advice was of no value to me prior to his death. The words that were spoken helped prepare me for what was about to become my new chapter in life. These seven words freed me: "There is no wrong way to grieve." Those words liberated me for the journey ahead and all the emotions that I had no idea I would feel. Wow! That was it! The value of those words sank into my mind, and I recalled them anytime I was told by someone that I had grieved long enough or that it did not take all that. Oh really? So, tell me something! How would you know? That type of statement usually comes from a person who has not experienced the loss of a close family member. That is something to ponder, isn't it?

"THERE IS NO WRONG WAY TO GRIEVE" NOTE PAGE

It is important to express how you feel so you can start processing your grief.

Write seven words that describe your initial feeling when your loved one passed away:

1. ______________________________

2. ______________________________

3. ______________________________

4. ______________________________

5. ______________________________

6. ______________________________

7. ______________________________

UNANSWERED QUESTIONS

I had questions, and I needed some answers so I could walk through the levels of grief that I was feeling such as shock, denial, pain, anger, sadness, numbness, blame, depression, uncertainty, acceptance, letting go, fear. Do you recognize all of this?

All I kept saying to myself was, “Wesley, you promised me that you wouldn't leave me, and you left anyway. Lord why did you take him from me and why now?” So, I was mad at Wesley for leaving, and my anger was directed at God for taking him! If there is one thing I know, it's that God doesn't owe us any explanations. He can do whatever He wants whenever He wants to do it. God is sovereign.

“So, God, how about I just push you away? Since you took Wesley, I do not have to let you into that space that is broken, crushed, and in pain because it hurts too much. I will show you God! You took my husband, so I won’t let you in!” Okay, I just discerned the expression on your face that says, “She can’t say and do that!”

Well, I did because that is how I was feeling at the moment. Remember those seven words? “There is no wrong way to grieve.” I was angry. I was mad, and it is through those expressions not the lack thereof, that people are able to release how they feel and what they are thinking. No, I did not stop loving God whom I'd been serving for more than 50 years when my husband transitioned. However, my Holy Ghost was not on display, my feelings were! I had to be honest and transparent enough to deal with every emotion that I was faced with - good, bad, or ugly! This was part of the process that was necessary as I began the steps of healing.

I was not trying to prove to anyone that I was strong. The truth was I was vulnerable and helpless, and even though I would not let God in, He never shut me out! Wow! He did understand where I was at that time.

He could relate to the feelings I was experiencing! I could talk to Him! I could cry and scream, if need be, and He would not leave me nor forsake me! He was still there to catch me when I was ready to be caught. That is when I realized that it was time for me to allow God in so that He could get me through the process of healing - so I could keep living. Yes, I said to keep living. There were times that my will to live waivered.

If you recall earlier in this book, there were five questions that I mentioned as layers of healing. Let's revisit them, but I'm going to answer them in a different order.

Why did Wesley leave me?

After a loss, as time goes by there are questions that a person may not be ready to deal with right away. The loss is still too fresh, and the wounded individual might not be comfortable addressing certain thoughts and/or subjects. I recall there were times when I would be talking with my husband and all of a sudden, I would start crying and say to him, “Wesley, don’t you leave me!” Of course, his reply was always, “Baby, I’m not leaving you. I’m not going anywhere.” He would do his best to reassure me and dismiss my fears. Yes, my fears. Job says, “What I have feared has now happened to me. What I dreaded has come true.” (Job 3:25-26) What a true scripture.

Some circumstances can be fueled by a person’s own fears. However, I believe more than my fears, the Holy Spirit was trying to prepare me for his exit. I wasn’t ready to hear that nor to accept it. As I look back, I can now see that Wesley’s departure was not pre-mature. That leads me to my second question.

Why did God take him from me?

I am understanding some things better as I get older. One of those things is that God sees,
and I believe He also feels the love, devotion, joy, peace, and happiness that exists when our
loved ones are close, near and dear to us. Family is important to God. The bond and love of

family falls right under our love for God. However, that doesn't erase God's Sovereignty.
(Eccles. 3:1-2a) "To everything there is a season and a time to every purpose under heaven. (2a) A time to be born and a time to die;" As I began to reflect on all of the things that Wesley had been - a caring son, a faithful and loving husband, a protective and nurturing natural father; a spiritual father, a loyal and devoted pastor - he emptied out everything to leave a memorable legacy, and it was his time to die. Lord I accept that now.

Could I have saved him?

This is a question that many people ask themselves after the person's departure. I began to revisit in my mind all the steps and what had taken place that Monday morning on May 21, 2012. I had to relive every moment so I could be certain that I had done everything in my ability to try and save my husband's life. I relived when I saw him sitting on the bed saying to me, "I can't breathe," to watching him being placed on the gurney as the paramedics took him out of our home and put him in the ambulance. When I got to the hospital to see Wesley, I was greeted by a woman whom I later found out was a chaplain. After being taken to a consultation room, I was informed by the on-call doctor that when Wesley arrived at the hospital, he had already stopped breathing. He had stopped breathing right before he was rolled out of the front door of our home.

They proceeded to try and resuscitate him all the way to the hospital, and there was no response. There was nothing I could have done to save his life. I had to accept that as well.

What will I do without Wesley?

Since our relationship was so great and we were just three months shy of celebrating our 40th wedding anniversary, that question carried a lot of weight for me! What was I going to do without my soul mate - my life partner? I didn't know. I only knew that this was the beginning of a journey that I had never taken, and I was going to need help to survive.

When we admit that we need help, I know for a fact that God will send the help, support system, and everything needed to take those difficult steps. He provided the help so at that point it was necessary for me to accept it. When the garage would go up, I would immediately think about Wesley, even though I knew he was gone. Seeing his shoes and clothes in the closet, the smell of his cologne, everything was still in place because it was too painful for me to move or throw anything away.

It took a while before I could even consider letting go of the things that represented who he was. These were tangible memories that kept him close to me. I cried myself to sleep many nights, still reminded of those words, "There is no wrong way to grieve." Every decision that I had made with him was now being made without him.

So How Do I Live Now?

There was one thing that my husband always did and that was to remind me that I was more than his wife and ministry partner. He continued to remind me that I should never forget about God's purpose for my life! That was already determined before he knew me, and it would be imperative that I fulfill purpose before leaving this earth. I am sharing this because as females, when we get married, if we are not careful, we will place our God-given purpose aside while fulfilling our assignments in ministry as wives and helpmates. Having a husband who wants to pull out of his wife what is already been placed in her is so vitally important. That is what Wesley always did for me. He would say, "God is not going to get me because you didn't do what He called you to do." Well, I don't believe he has to worry because he definitely did his part. He was my biggest supporter and cheerleader! We did not compete with each other; we completed each other! God knew exactly who I needed in my life and what a blessing he was to me in every way! To share our journey of almost 40 years of life would take another book.

Wesley fulfilled every God-given assignment over his life. He was happy, content, and favored by God, grooming many spiritual sons and daughters, and some are now pastoring, evangelizing and still walking with the Lord! So, in spite of the grief, I must live!
I must give myself permission to do so!

For so long I felt as if it was not fair for me to live since he was not here to live with me.
But not only is that not what God would expect of me, neither would Wesley want that for me. I remember at a very low time when I had a dream, and Wesley was in it. He was walking away from me as I tried to catch up with him. I was calling his name, but he never spoke or even turned to look in my direction. I finally got close enough to grab his hand, only for him to pull his hand away from mine. I immediately woke up and I heard these words, "You have work to finish. Fulfill your assignment!" I began to cry because at that time I did not want to hear those words! I wasn't ready to do that yet! It did not happen overnight. I eventually started taking small steps, moment by moment. I began to slowly embrace those words and other words of affirmation Wesley spoke to me. I remembered his positive attitude and confidence, seeing his hands folded as he peeked over his reading glasses with a smile of approval. Yes! I can do this! I must do this! I shall not die but LIVE and Declare the Works of the Lord! Psalm 118:17

"UNANSWERED QUESTIONS"
NOTE PAGE

Have you ever asked yourself, "Is this a dream, or are they really gone?"

Many questions begin to flood your memory. What questions have you asked yourself?

1. ____

2. ____

3. ____

4. ____

FACING A HURDLE

I had finally started returning to assisting in the care of my father. I had taken a 30-to-60-day break to reassess and to handle what was always *our* personal business that had now become *my* business. It was a bit strange at first.

Daddy's health was failing, and it was becoming more noticeable than before. I remember when I, along with my sons, went to see my dad the day after my husband transitioned. I needed to see my parents, but I needed to talk to my daddy. I needed to lean on him, cry, and hear him say to me, "You're going to be alright baby girl." It did not matter how old I was; it was comforting to know that I was still his baby girl. I could see the hurt in my dad's face as he tried to comfort me. Then he looked at me and he said, "Charlotte, before you make any major decisions be sure to talk it over with Wes, Jr., and Wayne, okay? Do you hear me?" Of course, I said, 'Yes daddy, I hear you."

As time went on, I was reminded of his words and his instructions as I sat next to his bedside. Outside of my husband, dad was always the other voice of reason for me. I never spoke to my sons about personal matters. So why didn't he include himself? He was not only my daddy, but a great pastor and a wonderful businessman. I wondered if dad was hiding something from me. He had already taken on the role of pastor emeritus and shifted some of his pastoral assignments to other ministers at the church. By this time, he had removed himself from being available for all important matters. He was still with us, but with his limited strength he was becoming content and at peace. So, when dad told me to do that, I didn't question him about it, nor at that time did it cross my mind to wonder why he hadn't said, "Come to me."

Later, it dawned on me that daddy knew he would soon be leaving us, so that is why he never said, "I'll be here for you daughter." When a person knows that he or she has emptied out, that person can be at peace, and that is how he was. Seven months after losing my husband, my dad transitioned peacefully.

How can a person heal from one loss when hit with another one within the same year? My husband and my dad were two of the most important men in my life, and they were both gone within such a short time of one another. "How do I move on from here? I need my husband! I need my daddy! Lord this is too much! I am still taking baby steps and trying to heal from the loss of my husband. So, it is hard for me to wrap my head around another loss," my emotions screamed.

Do you remember me saying there is no wrong way to grieve? Well, I am beginning to understand a bit more about what that means. In this life, when the unexpected comes our way, we may need to pause, think, or sometimes not think. Why? I am glad you asked. Because during the time of grief we will have important decisions to make that will ultimately affect us in the near future. So, one thing we should never do is act as if we have all the answers. That would be impossible to do for someone who has never encountered a loss that is so personal. I am grieving, yet I am not mentally ready to handle all these matters. I am working through the process, yet I do not have all the answers. And guess what! I found out while grieving that it is okay to say, "I don't know."

During my time of grief, I was running on autopilot, and that was getting me nowhere. I wasn't ready to accept the fact that Wesley was never coming back to me. I can hear someone thinking, "Aren't you a believer? Don't you know that death was not his end and that he will live again?" Well, let me help you. Yes, I know all the Biblical scriptural references related to living again.

"For we know that if our earthly house of this tabernacle were dissolved, we have a building of God, an house not made with hands, eternal in the heavens." (II Cor. 5:1)

"I have fought a good fight, I have finished my course, I have kept the faith; Henceforth there is laid up for me a crown of righteousness, which the Lord, the righteous judge shall give me at that day: and not me only, but unto all them also that love His appearing." (II Tim. 4:7-8)

These scriptures are comforting and reassuring. However, when a person is grieving, these scriptures will not take away the ache in your heart. The ache is still there, and the loss is still real. The grieving person is experiencing a reality.

I recall sitting in a church service sometime after Wesley had passed, and I was feeling so out of place. It was not the same no matter how hard I tried to feel alright. I was not alright. Another autopilot playback moment. Me? Yes me - the pastor's widower, the evangelist, the saved tongue-talking one! I felt so out of place that I just wanted to exit the building, get in my car, and drive, drive, and keep driving. I did not care or know where; I just knew I needed to leave and get away. I was so overwhelmed with grief, sorrow, anger, and abandonment. The only thing that stopped me from getting to the exit door was that my son saw me heading out the sanctuary.

He saw the look in my eyes from a distance and ran over to me, held me, and said these words, "Mom, it's gonna be alright. I've got you." All I could do was release a loud scream! That is when I knew that in time, not right away, but in time, I would make it. There was no rush. I just needed time.

I wish I could explain to you how it feels when it seems like not even God can help. All I can compare it to is the feeling that someone had taken away half of my heart and I was struggling to live. It is not easy. When a spouse, a child, even a parent is lost, there seems to be no earthly replacement.

However, I will say this: It is at those times when the word of God becomes life. When it is understood that the effectual fervent prayers of the righteous availeth much. I had no doubt that it was the prayers of the righteous that were holding me together and keeping my mind. I cannot imagine not being covered and protected by the Lord Jesus Christ. I am a witness that He is truly a mind regulator! Thank you, Lord!

"FACING A HURDLE"
NOTE PAGE

"The Lord himself goes before you and will be with you; He will never leave you nor forsake you. Do not be afraid; do not be discouraged." *Deut 31:8 NIV*

Write seven words that describe your initial feeling when your loved one passed away:

1. ______________________________

2. ______________________________

3. ______________________________

4. ______________________________

5. ______________________________

6. ______________________________

7. ______________________________

THE UNEXPECTED HAPPENS

It had been a while since Wes and Dad had left us. I was thanking God that Mom was still with us. She and Daddy were married for more than 65 years when he transitioned, so if Mom could hold on, surely, I could, too.

It was obvious that Mom was missing his presence so very much. I would go to the house and spend hours with her talking, laughing, and enjoying her company. It was such a delight! However, in the midst of that, our eldest son was in remission from a serious illness. So, my time and thoughts were occupied with visits to my mom and periodically my son. Being occupied does not mean healing. Sometimes, it becomes a mental escape for a period of time. Yet, at the end of the day, when the crowd dwindled, when the family members were no longer around and I had to go home alone, I then had to face the reality of those who were no longer here with me. It hurt not hearing Wesley's voice nor seeing his handsome face and not being able to talk to my dad on the phone daily; just my thoughts and me. My memories of what was and would never again be, was the only thing I could hold on to.

It was so refreshing to have the support of my sons, my daughters-in-love, and my grandchildren. Family is a precious commodity, and sometimes that is not realized until some family members start slipping away. We have always had a large community of loved ones. We would meet on every holiday at the "Thompson Mansion." It was our meeting place. There was always traffic in and out of the family home. There was a large, outside space, a basketball court, a game room inside the home, and enough space inside to just sit and talk to one another. As I am reminded, I see the many faces of family members who visited there and deposited good things into my life as I was growing up and into the lives of my children.

Change was not easy. Dad was no longer with us. However, it was still important that we maintained the family connection, not only for us, but for Mom. She had lost her husband of 65+ years. Dad and Mom were used to daily hearing the voices of loved ones, the sound of televisions, laughter, the grands, and great grands coming into their room talking to them. There was always a lot of action and traffic at the Thompson's Mansion. These were the things that needed to remain to keep mom lively and living!

As the new year approached, we had family gatherings to focus on. Even though I was still grieving the loss of my husband, I kept myself busy so I wouldn't have to put so much energy into thinking about it - at least not all the time. You might be saying, it sounds like you were still on 'auto-pilot'. And yes, looking back I would have to agree. I did my best to get out of the house most of the time. I was going to spend time with my Mom almost every day and to help care for her. Even running errands for her and getting her out of her home...I kept myself occupied.

Mom loved listening to gospel music! So, of course, when I would enter her bedroom suite, she would be sitting quietly on her couch, singing, rocking, and sometimes clapping her hands. I cannot imagine the level of emptiness she must have been feeling. Dad and Mom's years together were more than my age. It allowed me to realize that even when you have experienced something similar to another person's experience, your experience is still your own. Yes, I lost my husband, too, but my loss was not to be compared with hers. Dad was Mom's 'earthly' everything! He took her everywhere she wanted or needed to go. He cooked for her. Mom's sight had diminished over time, so she was no longer permitted to drive. Her lack of clear vision also contributed to her not being able to cook like she used to do. They were such a beautiful couple and loving example for all of us. I could see by the look in her eyes that she felt lost without her one and only. At times as she was listening to the music a tear or so would drop from her eyes. I recognized that at those moments he was probably strongly on her mind. I would either embrace her or hold her hand. It wasn't that she needed me to speak; she just needed to be comforted. Now that, I could understand and relate to. Sometimes, words are not what needs to be spoken during the grieving process. Can and will you embrace me, hold my hand, pray for me?

For some, this doesn't seem like enough. However, for those of us who are grieving, this is exactly all we are needing at that time. If words are spoken in their presence, keep it simple. “I love you. I am here for you. If you need anything, I will avail myself to you.”

It is also good to call the person and check on him or her from time to time. Do not say, “Call me if you need me,” because they won’t! The supportive friend or family member should initiate connection. If they do not pick up the phone, be sure to leave a message that is short yet to the point. I cannot even begin to tell you how these types of interactions got me through some of my darkest moments. For friends and loved ones to be intentional during the grieving process is a must. Remember, it is a process, and it will take time, so don’t let anyone rush the process.

As time progressed, our mom began to experience dementia. There were times she knew me as her daughter, Charlotte, and would call me by my name. Then there were times when she referred to me as, “that other lady.” My sister and I would laugh about it during our private conversations with one another. However, deep inside it saddened us to see how she was becoming more and more disconnected from the present world of reality and slipping back into her past. She was still seeing all our faces coming and going through the house, yet she could not connect us to her as her family. Her short-term memory was slowly leaving. I had lost my husband and father in the same year. Was I going to lose my mom, too?

Do you remember me mentioning my oldest son, Wesley Jr.? Well, he, his wife, Renetia, and their family happened to be living with us when my husband, Wesley, transitioned. Since my son was in remission and was doing fine, they were able to move, get their own place and start moving forward as a healthy family!

I was so happy for them. It had been a long journey, but God! As I mentioned before, along with my daily visits to see Mom, I would also go visit Wesley Jr., checking on him to see how he was progressing. He was looking good; he was driving again! Being able to spend quality time with his wife and three small children was priceless. Every time I was able to see my son, I thanked God for sparing his life!

I still had both of my sons, beautiful daughters in-love, five grandchildren and one additional grand coming soon! God was good to me. I found no fault in Him! We welcomed our newest addition into the family in January 2013! There were many challenges with his birth, yet he made it here! We had been through a lot as a family, and with God's help we would get through this! Christian was given his Papa's middle name, Adell. He had never met him, yet we could see many similarities. Christian Adell Moore, Wayne and Carissa's baby boy. I won't share the challenges that this child has been through, but I will share this; Christian is our miracle child. He is a living testimony!

We were all moving forward. I was still going through the process. It had been a little over a year since Wesley's transition in May of 2012 and dad's passing in December of the same year. I had to stay busy to keep from breaking down and either crying or screaming! The love and support received were overwhelming, in a good way. And I can honestly say that no one was rushing me to get over it. That is another phrase that people should never say to a person who is grieving. Besides, what does, "get over it," mean? It's like telling someone to either forget about the person or to forget about his or her passing. Neither sounds good to me.

As we progressed into the year 2013, Wesley, Jr. began to experience some health complications which meant he would need to have another surgery. "Okay, we've got this! He's going to be just fine," I thought.

It was so wonderful being able to see Wesley bond with his family again. Renetia and the children were happy to be in their own living quarters. There was some normalcy taking place in their lives.

From time to time, I would go by their home during the day and visit with my son, watching the faces of my grandchildren being overjoyed because Daddy was getting better!

I remember when he had to go in the hospital for a few days, I would visit him daily and read to him. I would pray with him and sometimes sing with him. Since he was a psalmist and a worshipper, Wesley Jr. loved singing praises unto the Lord. It was so beautiful to be able to spend quality time with my oldest son. I would always leave the hospital feeling encouraged and confident that Wes was improving and happy about his future.

His surgery was scheduled for August of 2013. After surgery, Wesley came home from the hospital to start healing. As time went by, however, there were some unexpected health complications that arose. Two months later, on October 28, which was one day after his father's birthday, Wesley Jr transitioned.

"When my heart is overwhelmed lead: me to the Rock that is higher than I."
Psalm 61:2 KJV

ANOTHER HIT

So, how was I to handle this and grieve properly when there was another loss - this time, my son? There are things that happen in life that hit so hard that it is difficult to comprehend or to explain with words. I was numb, still operating on autopilot. I do believe there was one thing a grieving person should never do and that is to say within yourself, "I have to keep moving for my family." What is wrong with that statement? It gives the illusion that one must be strong for everyone else even when he or she cannot be. Having that thought pattern will not allow a person to grieve or to heal properly. You may not like what I am about to say, but I need to say this: We are not capable of being strong for everyone else. That is not our job! We are not their God!

Whoa! Did I just say that? I most certainly did! If you are grieving, stop putting unreasonable expectations on yourself for the sake of others. If not, you will hide under the disguise of those famous words, "I'm okay." Pull away and give yourself permission to grieve so you will one day be strong enough to live.

It had been three years since the transition of my son, and we were watching Mom sink deeper into the stages of dementia. The only person that she recognized and called by name was my sister. She had started referring to me as, "that nice lady" who came by daily to help her and talk to her. There is nothing worse than to watch your parent slowly slip away. Mom was here, but she wasn't really with us. I didn't like that for us, but especially not for her. Yet it was refreshing whenever I arrived at the house, walked into her bedroom, and would see her sitting on her lounge sofa. She would be humming and singing along with the gospel songs. She would smile at me kindly as I kissed her on the forehead. Even though she was mentally at a distance, still having her here meant so much to me.

Ecclesiastes 3:1 reminds me that, "To everything there is a season, and a time to every purpose under the heaven." We want our loved ones to remain with us forever or maybe that's just me. However, that's not reality because there is a time to every purpose under the heaven. Even death has a time and purpose. It hurt to see her unsure of everything and looking at Daddy's picture, knowing that he was no longer here. She was the one who I knew was praying for me, covering me, and supporting me. My mommy taught me how to be a proper young lady, even what was appropriate to wear as a woman. She later showed me how to be a good wife, a caring mother, and a First Lady.

Through her showing me, she was always teaching. She was my mom and mentor - my midwife. What a blessing!

Ecclesiastes 3:2 says, "A time to be born, and a time to die; a time to plant, and a time to pluck up that which is planted;" I don't believe anyone is ever ready for a loved one to leave this earth. Our attachment to them is personal and many times selfish. We forget that they are only meant to be with us for a season because we all have an appointment with death, according to Hebrews 9:27. On March 28, 2016, the day after Resurrection Sunday, Mom had her appointment. It was her time to die and the time to pluck up that which had been planted.

"But thou, O Lord, art a shield for me; my glory, and the lifter up of mine head."
Psalm 3:3 KJV

It is so easy to push things to the background while other circumstances and situations start to become a priority. So, what about the loss of loved ones? How is life to be balanced in the midst of grief, or should balance not be a goal while grieving? My husband, Wesley, passed away suddenly in May of 2012, and then just seven months later, in December of 2012 my father transitioned. In October of 2013 my son, Wesley Jr., died. How does one cope with multiple deaths within their family circle? I became a widow after 39 years of marriage; my Mom after 65 years, and Renetia after 9 years. None of us were totally prepared, and we were each thrust into a new normal at different ages.

My heart grieved for my mom when Daddy transitioned, thinking about how it would affect her. She was much older than I was. They were like a pair of shoes. No one buys one shoe. They come in pairs. Then my heart was also heavy for my daughter-in-love. A young widow with three small children to raise. It just did not seem fair at all. Even being filled with the spirit of God, we must never push back and ignore our human side. When we do so, we cannot properly heal.

It just so happened that while Mom was still with us, I had signed up with a biblical counseling group that I believed would spiritually and mentally assist me regarding the passing of both Wesley and Daddy. Yes, you read it right - spiritual and mental help. As believers, we must be transparent with God. Yes, he already knows where we are and what we are lacking. However, he needs us to confess that thing with our own mouths. Unfortunately, we are not all doing that, which contributes to the delay of our healthy healing so that we can have a balanced life.

As we were getting down to the final counseling sessions, that's when Mom became physically challenged along with other health difficulties which resulted in her transition. Therefore, her death at that time, was also unexpected. It was when my mom passed that I was finally able to grieve the passing of my husband, my dad, and my son. I was even able to receive some counseling that walked me through my deepest and most vulnerable moments. Did my mother's death honestly release all of what I had been holding on to and hiding from? Perhaps that is possible. All I know is that it was as if a breaking took place in me, both spiritually and naturally. I was beginning to feel a freedom I had not felt since May 21, 2012, and from that day forward I had been putting walls up and subconsciously shutting God out.

There is never a replacement for the healing spirit of the Lord. However, there are certified and licensed people who specialize in fields that can assist us naturally, so we will not roll over and stop in our tracks. I am grateful for the support I received both naturally, mentally, and spiritually. I thank God that through this process my complete healing had finally begun.

It's been quite a few years now, and every time I visit a place that is connected to one of my loved ones who has transitioned, there's a trigger, a subtle reminder of the way things used to be - a favorite shopping spot with mom, dad's laughter and our lengthy conversations over the phone, hearing my son's worship song, our favorite family restaurant, loving conversations with my husband and his embrace that reassured me that all was well. I do not believe that any of this will ever fade away, and it shouldn't. There are so many great memories that keep me smiling when I think about each one of them because they are all a part of my life. Each, in their own way, has helped to shape the person I have become. We don't forget. We choose to move on. This is what our loved ones would want us to do. That is why unapologetically, I give myself permission to LIVE! And it is time for you to start doing the same!

Will it be easy? Not at first, and it may take a while to adjust to your new norm. However, it is important that you have a good community circle of people (family and friends) who will keep you engaged so you do not disconnect with the real world.

Your loss has left your heart shattered. It has been devastating and a difficult thing to comprehend. That is why having the right people in your life during this time is so crucial. You may not be able to see how you are even able to go forward. So, allow me to speak from my own difficult experiences and say that you can, and you shall survive!

Yes, there is life after, so go ahead! Speak to yourself and say these words: “From this day forward I will **give myself permission to Live**!”

"The LORD is my strength and my shield;
My heart trusted in him, and I am helped:
Therefore, my heart greatly rejoiceth;
And with my song will I praise him."
Psalm 28:7

Thank You!

I want to thank you for your investment. It is my prayer that you have been helped in some way by reading my life's journey. No matter where you are right now in your stage of grief, continue to take each day moment by moment. God is with you, and He is your strength. He will carry you through every pitfall, every valley, and get you to the top of the mountain! Your valley experience will soon be a mountain top Victory!

Until the next book, stay encouraged and when no one is around, be reminded that I am praying for You!

Your Sister in Christ,

Charlotte

An Overcomer!

#ExpectMoore

Contact Information:

Charlotte Moore
charlotte@called2nations.org
www.called2nations.org

THERE IS HEALING

And Life After

AFFIRMATION

I am a child of God who is loved and never forsaken nor forgotten. My life is safe in the hands of my Father. He has promised to always provide all I will ever need. I trust Him with all that concerns me. The love of the Father abides in me.

I Corinthians 13:4-8a

4 Charity suffereth long and is kind; charity envieth
not; charity vaunteth not itself, is not puffed up 5
Doth not behave itself unseemly, seeketh not her
own, is not easily provoked, thinketh no evil, 6
Rejoiceth not in iniquity, but rejoiceth in the truth; 7
Beareth all things, believeth all things, hopeth all
things, endureth all things. 8a Charity never fails.

THOUGHTS AND MEMORIES

www.ingramcontent.com/pod-product-compliance
Lightning Source LLC
LaVergne TN
LVHW050427160826
845677LV00002BA/582

* 9 7 9 8 9 8 5 1 5 4 4 1 2 *